*Dire Straits*

by Edward Foster

Poetry

*Edward Foster*

# Dire Straits

Marsh Hawk Press • East Rockaway, NY • 2012

12 13 14 15 7 6 5 4 3 2 1 FIRST EDITION

Marsh Hawk Press books are published by Poetry Mailing List, Inc., a not-forprofit
corporation under section 501(c)3 United States Internal Revenue Code.
Printed in the United States of America.

Text: Goudy Old Style
Titles: Palazzo

*The author is grateful to Lisa Bourbeau, Joseph Donahue, Leonard Schwartz,
and Susan Terris for their advice and support in the preparation of this book.*

Library of Congress Cataloging-in-Publication Data

Foster, Edward Halsey.
   Dire straits / by Edward Foster. ~ 1st ed.
     p. cm.
   Poems.
   ISBN 978-0-9846353-8-2 (pbk.) ~ ISBN 0-9846353-8-6 (pbk.)
   I. Title.
   PS3556.O7592D57 2012
   811'.54~dc23
                        2012013250

Marsh Hawk Press
P.O. Box 206, East Rockaway, N.Y. 11518-0206
mheditor@marshhawkpress.org

*In memory of Andrei Tarkovsky*

———

"And what is the life of this world except the enjoyment of delusion."
—*Qur'an* 3; 185 (translation: Saheeh International)

# Contents

Photographs: Front cover: St. Petersburg, Russia — p. 4: top, Clarence; bottom, the Süleymaniye, Istanbul — p. 10: top, Jersey City, N.J.; bottom, Mt. Monadnock, N.H. — p. 17: top, Deerfield, Mass; bottom, Greenfield, Mass. — p. 26: top, Charlemont, Mass.; bottom, Greenfield, Mass. — p. 34: top, Arusha, Tanzania; bottom, Washington, D.C. — p. 42: top and bottom, Addis Ababa, Ethiopia — p. 50: top, Quaker meeting house, Adams, Mass.; bottom, Arusha, Tanzania — p. 59: top, Northampton, Mass.; bottom Ngorongoro Crater; p. 68: top, Oakland, Cal.; bottom, Jersey City, N.J.; p. 74: top, Saugerties, N.Y.; bottom, Istanbul — p. 82: top, Greenfield, Mass.; bottom, Ankara

*Dire Straits*

# A Drawer Full of Glass Slippers;
## or, Those Who Can, Choose

We tried to patronize your fame
because we knew you'd find a way
to set ambition, your ambition,
down in verse.

You were born to rule,
had parents, wealthy folk,
and they were good.

They let you read the books you should,
have jobs that no one understood
but you.

Tenuous but firm,
you spoke your piece,
drew your breath,
and smiled.

No one understood
exactly what you meant,
but you won prizes.

We think that folks like you
deserve to be received
with honors
the rest of us
don't want.

## And He Said

1.
And in this reverie, my lover,
rolling over,
said,
"Try to get along with other men."
(No cadence, no inflection, flat.)

He meant their plans.
"You did not make the world.
They didn't make the world for you."

I stand corrected.

2.
You're a flimsy person at this point,
at any point with him:
old metaphors, weak body,
soft intent. Watch me dance.

Did you notice how the young men looked today?
Never use such words with them.
Learn their lesson, but find contagion
in another eye, any eye.

# Angelic Concerns for the Rosy Swan, a Bar,

which I have never seen
but dreamt, for there
folks are friends,
the kind who face each other
at the dawn
in bed, and not alone.

\*

My erstwhile friend took classes
in constructing verse,
where teachers praise,
though fellow students
criticize this line or that
and wonder if he's
"earned that final line."

\*

In my dream,
these people tease
their fame.

\*

My friend that was
won't join them
for he hates their sound,

writes verse
supple as my leather and his skin,
in which he finds a pleasure.

## BACK TO MIKE

If you became invisible,
would he like you more?
That way he might read into
empty space
just what he needs.

He might see in you an old gazelle
or dancing bears
on ice floes in the cold.

Anything he'd want.
You could roar or
humbly kiss his wedding ring,
                    if that would do.

And then expect
that when the sky is dark,
he'd return to you.

## Bagno Vignoni with the Pope

Without intent: my loss,
giving up what makes
one poor, as poor as Francis.

Quiet cloaks your
face until the light turns on:
a false light, no illumination from within.

Then can you say your freedom's
won? You're chosen,
like the lords
of finance,
ones who cloak
disgust as politics.

The men who lead
are hiding,
but they know success.

BAKST

Whom do we listen for?
If she could be heard,
would she bring the curtain
(and all this searching)
down?
Could she end the show
the way Bakst did
despite his work (to make
his master proud)
and then was
shunt aside?

What became of him?
Should we write histories
of men whose learning
disappeared?

## BIG DIOMEDE

Looking for the Moscow
check-in booth,
I saw such lovely men
I fell in love
seven times.

The airport turned
a brilliant blue.

      *

Not one of them
knew
what I had seen
in them.
I wish those men
had all seen me
and liked the view.

      *

But no, just haze and rush
until the agent
at the counter looked askew.
She studied me.

She'd seen my eyes flash blue.
I knew she knew too much.

## CHASING THE WIND

You know the rules

after they change,
when the old are young again.

The image is mine:
care calls for him.

## Computer with an Erstwhile Friend, Late

Terminal (end light
passing through) . . .
and then he told me
(I, looking ridiculous,
as always):
sing,
as if that would do.

"Isn't that what poets do?" he said.
In fact, that's not what poets do
today, nor do they (as his second guess)
just play with words
as if each poem were a game,
precurser of his internet.

I have a feeling he has
no favored word.

            *


Excuse me, Bob.
I need to work.

# Dancing with Cole

Can you get pianos with just his notes?
They're different, like the soundings
that attract
your anxious grace.

If not,
please leave and
close the door.
Forget his eager sound.

The notes he's told to play
are his alone.

# Donskoy Monastery and the Tourist

Where were they shot?
Show me where. Or describe the spot.
Also let me know where they were burned
and how their comrades lit the fire
and justified their act.
It's a place I need to see.

I've never seen such gloom.
No tears. I'm looking out this window,
and it's cold. Would you like to look?
Perhaps you'd like to look for me.

Nothing fits, though horror
happened here. Is there anywhere
its secret can't be known?
Keep your balance.

## Double Blind

The rainbow
holds his bud,
his flourishing.

The blind man
comes to us
but won't believe.
His images are
measurements,
forever new.
He is a franchise,
franchising self.
Born an engineer,
he flourished long ago,
before the rain,
before the flood,
before he hid
within the ark.

His covenant:
"Be happy, soulless.
Measure inclination, amusement,
the distance to my bed."

"How fast I go," he says, running.

                *


That man's a dragon,
a cache of calculations,
and limitless delays.

Yet just this once,
he hopes you'll
spend the night.

## Having a Drink Alone

They've chosen not to hear
and do not know you stand above.

They have a celebration.
You watch them from your balcony.
The air is hot.
You can't retreat.

Enamored, you'd
close out the sound,
and close the door.
Imaginary windows
will not shut.

The happy ones you're watching, leave.
The joy you heard from them
is gone.
Why did they acquiesce?
Why did they do what others want?

Perhaps it gave them joy.

                    *


Every evening there are more to see.
You see them passing down below.
You cannot close the door.
The windows will not shut.
You wonder how they pass the night.

# HE SHARES A JOKE WITH GOD

"The really terrible thing is that everyone has his reasons." —Jean Renoir, *The Rules of the Game*

The king you are pretends you have the look,
watching how the folds of clothing curve:
they're sleek and blue.
Memories of war return.

"I'm your poet," you advance.
"You have my kingdom. Fellows watch,
and everything's the way it's always been,
        much as you want."

"Oh, don't you like to end this way?" you ask.
Well, neither does your correspondent,
who fits inside your skin and moves about,
measuring your inches,
the way you rule.

## Her Diaspora

Not to know. Never to obey.
Self-appointed, she
has crossed the sea
for her Parisian holiday.

She lifts her pen
to write a final correspondence
within her universe
of doubt.

Closets are the kindest place
for poets such as she,
living deep in unacknowledged
diffidence,
up late.

Thoughts swarm in reverie.
Abstractions empty.
Objects stand and serve
no need.
She leaves her figurines
dishonored in new languages
she thinks could live.

No, this once gentle mind
can't respond.
We recall when
all the artificial lights
went out, and she was left
alone
in bed with acid dreams
she'd perpetrate.

In this, her frenzy
had to fail.

Disobedient in social norms,
she followed those
who cheer as one. Charisma
doesn't count in words if
their loud cheering stops.

# His Fetish and What It Did for Me

"I can't keep my eyes off her kneecaps." —inscribed on a student's desk

Students, please be serious:

Look at that object in quiet. Your eyes cannot move. You cannot touch. You cannot touch it. You can touch nothing. Close your eyes. Do not imagine what you have seen. Do not think that you see it, and you will find what you have always known.

Photographs contain nothing: not the child who screams, not the delicate lady who washes her arms in the lake.

The shape of the man who walks toward you at last, is gone.

Your eyes water as you watch again the light. Here is the failure of all friends, the necessary failure that must always be. All that you were taught.

Does a word fascinate when its image is gone?

# Hive Mentality

Reverse the platitudes of those
who think they own the words
and make things out of them,
shifting syllables left or right,
giving credence to distraught
and fearsome thoughts (as if
they were young boys, quite free,
riding bikes in traffic).

There's no destination in these Persian
lands of wandering bards, clichés
we had to learn. Why poke among
old languages in search of something
new? All I need is you, your slick-backed
hair to paralyze my thought,
hard grasping you.

# HOPE DASHED AGAIN

I want to give you
all you came to find:
all the rushes from
unfinished films,
their busyness.

                    *

Each one's
a little script
that makes you feel
the gist
of what
the actors
elsewhere
say.

                    *

We bend down,
humbled
by their rigid revelation.
We take our seats.

                    *

Directors make us rush
through sequences
they say are
life itself.

                    *

Elsewhere,
professors of the body
gather,
collate
so-called elements
of life.

\*

We wish to dominate (all of us)
our meaning and our place.

\*

How much I'd like to give at least
a part
of what you came to find.

\*

But as it is,
words
can't
make this,
or any,
sequence
free.

26

# I KNOW NO LAW OR KINGS
*for Roy and Chris*

All we've seen on African plains
might be asked of Tarkovsky,
films of motion, inner war in color,
trains that blur and blur again.
(As we said. . . . So we heard . . . .)

Supple plains with water,
lions in the grass. Out of
Africa: enough for measure.
Nothing to hold: nothing made
to wish or keep.

Do not see beyond that line.
Sacrifice survival for that frame,
that limit, lions in the grass.
Out of Africa: see impediments,
an excuse, unneeded need.

Correspond with nothing:
its pleasures do suffice,
knowing neither law nor kings,
accepting light,
praise each flash.

## It's How You Dress

Half-way to heaven,
every time
youth will bring you down.
Now, tell me how the very touch of cloth
has weakened you. Somewhere in the valley,
Peter preaches his new gospel of fame,
for he is there: made it, climbed the ladder,
didn't fall. The grey of winter's lead did not
transport the dead. The awful revelation
was not told, yet Peter pushed us on
to be like him.

Tell me: Why arranging that blue cloth
about your body, frame, can weaken
me or send me to your ladder. —
Ecstasy's the servant that lets young
feelings roil in expectation: emotion
as a false light failing. Therefore,
you disabuse the sun and in no shadow
search for your salvation. Reason knows
it has no end,

and no "perhaps,"
but in locked rooms release
what wives and guardians ask
that we repress. Remember that sad teacher
thinking he had found the way
through talk. He hadn't even found
the first rung up.

Let me run my fingers on your loins;
cotton meshwork is your ploy.

# Language

I'm watching what he wears,
as do you, differently, recalling
styles that once transformed
the night. We recall black jackets
that, from films,
we learned to seek.
We heard
motors starting
in the dark and snow.

We know him now,
dressed as that one there:
a tyranny in black;
my soul is swept aside.

What does it mean? What
do we recall? Could
you ask questions
shaped the way we dress?

Sit closely.
Answer why,
as a child,
you never
asked where words begin.

To be intimate
means
not to know.

## LAWS OF THE GOLDEN DISK
### *(with thanks to Aleister Crowley)*

Let's make our prison
from the color red.

Would you heed me there?
Would I heed you?

I know your mountaintop, your fame,
has made you circumspect.

All those obligations
were the dance we had to do.

I hardly finished one
before another
brought me down.

Redness wasn't made for two,
when one is you.

## Limiting Choice

At first, he felt it might go smoothly like a film,
one take, or so it seemed,
though looking at the frames he shot, I saw
a multitude of shots, layered, none at rest,
much like a hive of insects rising from the ground,
moving all together, as a surface blurred.

                    In this film,
the sun would shine, children would arise
(part of all the smoothly felt) and leave.
The blessed part, the full grown man,
would never stay. You only had the screen
to touch, a bed of insects over which to
exercise control, in which to roll your hands.

## Locked In

The wrong broke loose,
yet you congratulate yourself.
Words pain and
comfort you. Comfort is the evil that
you want: to have no worry and
no wonder, no space for mirrors,
self, or neighbors looking in.

Do they see? Can they know
what we've been doing
here behind the blinds?
They have their husbands, wives,
no sense of being
in the world *alone*. Sleeping late,
reading with the children, dressing
with the children. Why don't the sacred
care? We're asked to share what little
lies so still, hidden by the walls.

We must be grateful for the walls.

# MARKET FORCES

She sits within her kitchen,
which she's always felt was hers.
She gathers grains of salt
and makes a little pile.
This much she also owns
but can't quite say the same
about the way she feels.

She watches leaves beside the window.
Spring is flourishing.
She feels her fingers move along
her old formica, clean.

# Memory in Red

Choose colors to format an image.
See it as red, install delight, so that
with the fullness of sin, the angel
(fully ours)
cuts a swath through flesh.

And now the blood can flow.

Then conjoin: images, hands, the color red.
How did we lose our faith?
Not lost: it fortifies our reason,
whose hand can only bandage
the swath within our flesh.

We proclaim our fortress and our strength,
undone and shut:
portcullis, sentiment, red.
Can we, please, forget to know?

## Money in the West

This endless project's nothing
but a river in the sand, a white
silt stream running through the West.
Death Valley's where we left
our child to rust in sand.
Who needs development?
Our nation's on the watch.
Each word is broad enough
for memory. Police will come.
The law will bring us down,
take life apart, and set us in
a landscape made wholly
out of rust.

# Mr. Wonderful

Allowed, forgone:
a quiet flaw, and wonder:
none. So he
embraces solitude.

There was a time when angling
for others kept him still.
Then everyone approved.
He knew America's polite.

Doctors beg their patients for disease,
teachers know their students never really know.
Lawyers seek their clients.

He was just a bureaucrat,
but a bureaucrat just the same,

listening to nothing others heard: vacuity,
violence, anger without a word,
no flourish,
nothing more.

You recall the helpless saint
he said he was. I would have
been that saint,
said foolish words
that I despise.

Yet eyes, dark blue,
hid his secret vice. Foolish words,
foolish wives, settled into childcare,
scrambled words, disappointment,
pretensions made of Greecian love
or anywhere he'd care to go.

## My Fingers

1.
Who are you to say
that there is little choice,
when other strangers tell
what's ours to see?
I watch you take
the easy road.
You're walking fast,
pretending this direction
is the one
you chose. What sense is there
if you use language only
to pretend intention,
things you mind?

When will I enter rooms
we can't discuss? I trusted
you, felt no sincerity, and dreamt
you empty. Early morning
showed us flowers
in the winter sun.
I fashioned you,
made arms, made touch,
somehow broke the crust,
came close.
The thing I touched was
you, only what I made.

You were the one I feared,
had costumes,
threatened night,
resisted need and emptiness.
What did I think I was
when I imagined touch
and you?

2.

Why assume when rain won't
come, I wouldn't stand
aside, alone? I watch
your face dissolve.
What's left is mine.

The wind will vanquish
if a man won't speak.
The rains will make it seem
that none was ever there.
Nothing owns this change.
Pride will flow in rivers
when you stop
and feel the waters washing
over you. That is the way I feel.
I run my fingers over flesh,
imagined flesh.

Lean close.

## MY HERO IN PRINT

His semblance is enough – acute –
the rains pass by – all things now
separate, broken, fragments, pretending to be whole.
I read his book – ignored his thought –
but keep his rhythm, cadence, sound.

What wonder stops his thought for me,
makes him seem apart,
alone?
          Long trails of
ego-centered love. Disease,
a new disease. His gestures
come to me
fraught with caution.

I fall asleep, fearful of an end
without a cause – performances
of lost delight,
reveries belonging
to a harmless grown-up child.

He has so much to tell,
this man, and I
am here alone to know it.

Move closer, where he is –
each word:
what did he sing before?

What's to salvage
from his syllables?
Why dissolve
his thought,
when he's so young?

## *NOSTALGHIA* IN TARKOVSKY'S WORLD

He is my shadow in the Roman baths,
where history is glitter and blood.
The woman is dead. Why did you
listen to her? What did she say?
Would she pleasure herself?
Or pleasure you? What is her secret?
Would you let yourself pause,
enveloped in sin?
The woman's alone. This woman
is dead. That madonna has failed,
as the caretaker said:
she cannot receive . . . as if
she had choice, as if you
had chance. This woman
is dead. She is alone,
though her shadow will remain.
She is gone.

## Nostalgia, To Be Alone

1.
Her time was open, unfixed,
the way all women ask to be seen
but rarely are. —

Listen to her heart as if that power
might reach another
as once it reached you.

2.
Carving fingers from stone and clay,
cleaving their image, it unfolds in the mind,
so that I reach and touch and lose control,
as if this life were knowledge,
collaborators sighing thoughts,
iridescent like the boys I've learned to love and shells.

## *NOTHUNG* IS A SWORD,

finality. Transposed,
you'll never be the sunrise
or the flesh that is
my luck. I prefer
to be your prophecy.
Lying still
is not enough.

*

Would you like to know
the simple secrets,
as I dress?
Of course, you don't.

*

Let us build a wall,
stone on stone.

*

You may cross
the wilderness,
and then can see
my house,
my bed.

*

You may enter.
You may share my meal.
You may share my bed.
But you can't touch me there,
nor will I you.

## Pensées

The opposition's getting strong.
I hear them throw their weight around.

All my life I tried, I really did.
The opposition's very strong.
I hear them lift the lid.

They look within.
I see them now.
I see them seeing me.

It's dark again.
I really did.

## Prohibitions

Sidle close. — Oh . . .
wary? Well,
so am I. And yet,

tonight
with us
this room reflected gold.

Peek out between the slats.
Watch the neighbors come and go.

Deserters, when there's war,
are shot or hung. I treat my prisoners
with kindness, though.

None of them is truly mine.

Examine what the neighbors see
when they look here.

You'd rather not?
I understand.
It's hard work
keeping secrets to one's self.

I sigh, and then:

Oh, stop your consternation.
Do you really think that you and I
are wanted anywhere?

None of us is special,
just weary.

## Secret Room

We have our sanctum,
idols moving in a row.
Our cave is nearly dark.
Outside the women pass the men
in search of them.

We cannot cross that border
We cannot leave this cave.
We cannot let the sunlight in.

Within our sanctum
we have made
a light

and furnished friends
with inner thought.
Refracting these,
we walk about the cave
and watch it glow.

## SETTING THE STAGE THAT IS NO STAGE

Colder than any day
so far:
at the side of the road,
all the fences,
only the snow,
nothing
to live with
in sight.

\*

Taking a minute,
let yourself know
there's no conclusion
you want.
Conclusions are all
we get, you and me,
our race of men,
dreading whatever the snow
may choose.

\*

Gentle, this man
becomes violent,
his face
stripping away
remnants of awe.

\*

We, too, know
violence
stripping away
remnants of awe.

*

I tell myself
I might drive home,
or leave the car and
disappear in snow.
The transit out of the self
none of us know,
but we can choose
the time.

*

The snow beyond the fence
is where we belong.

## Seven Coils: The Hangman's Noose

Why does it hurt?
The river runs without sound.
The birds in my sky do not sing.
Or cry.
The streets are quiet.
Empty. I have found
them neither bland, nor dark;
they hold us all,
unchanged, unchanging.
Why, then, does it hurt?

No thanks to myself,
or what I was taught:
was it a lie?

## SHALL WE BE JUST?

So you will find a way,
though you will not be heard.
You will sit in absence,
free to grasp:
credit, cash, things
made, like men,
to belong.

The evening is light.
It cannot be held.
You have lost so much.
Listen.

The claims to thought were false.
The voice was the voice of your mind,
the last of the vipers.
Salt waves would heal your wounds,
for in prison you are made to bleed.

False hopes
like the banks of a river
as the water runs high.
There is no truth,
you might easily say.

Why are you back?
What's left to mislead?
What is the gain?
There is no truth.

# SOLACE

The others were our given:
there is no solace now,
no search worth taking,
no knocking at the gate.

Our home is our refinement,
an image from the mind,
and friendship is the carriage
that jostles as we journey
to the sea.

The feckless child is ancient.
Our remaining days are few.
All this the others taught
before they left.

There is no solace now.

# THE COMPOSITE CHILD

Little B,
who says we beat him up,
which we did not,
welcomes home
no us.

For little B
conceives no sympathy
for selves like us
or other odd ones
strolling by.

"I'm only telling
what I saw," I say.
I saw you lift the veil.

(He smiles and walks away.)

Wait! I spoke too soon.
He has imaginary legions
ready at the gate,
preventing one and all
from knowing more
than what he would allow.

"Consider just the here and now,"
he says. "Poems cannot go beyond
what the senses know."

And yet they do:
"It's where they all begin," I say.
But he's in charge.

What happens
hardly matters,
yet we track him
to the brook
without respect
and hold him,
for a moment,
firmly,
in the dark.

"Give us answers,"
we intone,
for once the die is cast,
the die is cast.

We hold him to the ground.
We tell him, "Tell us
that you know you're wrong."
He moves his head
from side to side.

Lush summer grass,
brackish water in the brook,
flowing in the dark,
and language
teaching nothing
once the die is cast.

And so we (holding him)
carress his feckless face
as he recites his sins,
his many sins;
then we let him go.

## The Elderly Russian Starts To Dance *(The Youth Reflects)*

Denouncing all infirmity as if his seeds
weren't brown with age, and wrinkled,
their purpose in the world no longer known,
our guest begins to dance.
He holds no fiction,
makes no formula.

Pots and pans
ordered on the stove, the sink, behind
the doors. He had a mother, once.
Feelings then were plural. He keeps things
as they were.

He had his friends, elderly, obeyed.
The doors were shut, and old men
died. And then:
we pushed him from our midst.

## THE FROST

All this from wandering: the young boy that I am holds the stage
and dies. The trees will never blossom. The winter garden hides
it from my sight. Frost is greedy. Winter bears down the grass.
It infiltrates the attic of my home, solidifies the air,
enters my room. I hear it crack.

The walls are stone. Sickness is this moment.
How can I defend? The frost is in the furnace.
The frost becomes a human form. It enters rooms
as if to take another life. It's this revenge
that solitude has left behind.

# The Gift Giver: Tannhäuser

You are quite alone,
but syntax, moment,
time won't stop
until you make them stop.

Within her hill
she counts her vestiges
of grief.

Embarks within
new moments
to redeem
that grief.

Watch her clamber up
within her hill.

Listen to her thought.
She has secrets.

# THE GOLDEN DISK WITHIN MY SKIN

1.
The blessed angel unfolds within his rose.
Why, crouched within that bud, does
he avoid the sun?

                    The sun distracts.


An angel, he unfolds within the bud
and is my only sun.


The flower cannot see,
                    but he has eyes
on lips, on fingertips with which
he feels to see. The flower of the man
unfolds. I watch him reach,
                    so delicate,
                            and touch.


2.
But now, within another sleep,
taut within his bed,
he forfeits cause.
His solace is his need.


Is it revenge
that makes him
what I want?
For he is old.
He moves alone
among the sheets,
for he is nothing
to the one who was
his friend,
for he is old.

He is no less than
he might want,
but he is old.

3.
If I should live
within him now,
how would I be?

Age clutters mind
and fractures self
into a nebulae of touch.
I'd be his touch.

As such, his fringe becomes
my golden disk,
my star.
I am just as he'd wish, telling himself
that this prison, cell, this blanket of skin
holds me still.

It is the golden disk
he made
that holds me still.

# THE GREAT DOG FANG

He's gathered into folds of skin
such anger that we wish he'd go away.

Such truculence, you'd hardly guess
that he, this very morning,
had been thought the heaven's single star.

Making sympathy as once he could
with ease, such ease.

But now his furor binds him to a tale
of rancor, slick with spit.

Another tale was told about some girls
gone wild, doing vengeance,
breaking into homes, killing cats.

How sad to be alone. It makes
me start to think about such things
as girls gone mad.

"I'll show you,"
this he really said,
"I'll show just how angry I can be."

And so he did, but no:
No, dear.
There is no other you.

# THE HAUNTING

You've no idea
how much I've haunted you.
My cloak was night.
I read the books
you read, so
now you know
I know.

I saw the films you like.
I'd celebrate your holidays.
Your hair's too long,
your legs too short.
I made up compensations.

I overlooked the things
you wish you weren't.
You had another friend,
so close,
but I ignored this fact.

I ran my fingers
on your phantom back.
I run them still.
As such, I'm haunting you.

# THE LEAVES TURN YELLOW

then brown. We've deciphered
every cause, reason,
knowing that there is nothing
we cannot classify and know. And
yet the boy insists he'll have a holiday.
His friends and he would like to camp,
but sureness isn't all.
The weather could turn cold.
The winds might be unbearable.

Nothing you've achieved
can ever live again.

## THE MOVIE STAR

Distinguish personalities – and
       gratify yourself with less of
       life, compatriots who pleasure us.

Capacities dissolve –
       fragments have no independent life.
       They say but never say enough

to hold us in suspense. What next?
       The phone will ring.

Dissemble for your hero.
       Link his personality to light.

# THE SHUTTERED ROOM

*the orchard*
I try to find a moment where we're heard.
All differences distinct. You'd laugh.
The lane is open. We see it as if neither
you nor I had been a child.
So we pretend it's summer, and we touch
as in a film, you and I, beside this orchard,
down the hill from twilight,
seeking inner you.
                 We, in control,
remain unsatisfied. (No one in control is satisfied.)
Let the film run past the lens.
I am you, and you are on my arm.

*the room*
Such he told: this is what I am and
what I need. The room is shuttered
as I'd have it be. The furnishings
are old, but young men might be here,
though they aren't. They hold our strings
and threaten, with another laugh.
The light comes through in slivers,
and not one person's found.

*penetration*
He penetrates my fascination.
Intimacy, he argues, can't exist
in sheltered rooms. Let others watch:
solitude is proven by those who see,
and judge. It's all the way you write
the words you feel you have to write.
What you say is what the others watch.
To touch is this way felt.

*the film*
So you walk in and through his film,
framed indoors, with lights, flattened,
an illuminated screen, but none to watch —
knocking, asking who is there,
who's come, arrived? This way,
hiding in the shuttered room,
at home,
I'm never quite alone.

## The Smiling Folk

Smiling, and with little left to read,
the family goes to church.
Do they, this time, take another route?
In the lower forty-eight, we take our
knocks whichever way they come.
I'd almost welcomed hearing you,
but once again: no call. You
backed yourself
out of life.
The family won't be back.
They've learned a lesson no one
had to teach: they saw.
And here at home, there's none of us
on call. We might as well take refuge
in your drawing room: sitting back,
come and help us read another book.

# The Technocrat Makes a Prison Without Walls

We have no answers
in the vacuum built by aged men,
accentuating wealth.

No answers work.

I almost wish I'd joined them.
What's the sense of writing verse
in closets or underneath a quilt,
sublime with dark confessions
and a partial smile:
yes, folks, I did it.
I did it all.

Home is where they'll
never let you go,
those older men
who sever you from friendship,
regarding how you twist and turn
in chemical despair.

The dramas you conceive!
Dear engineer:
you do not care.

We caught this meaning
secreted by an older, richer class,
who built themselves a prison,
then a dozen more.

And then they said:
"Find one that comforts you.
Strong bars will keep us steady."

# The Woman with Writing on Her Back

"Treat me like the page of a book." —Nagiko in Peter Greenaway's *The Pillow Book*

I'm left to see her burn the books we wrote.
A leopard, fashioned in restraint,
she'll obligate another boy in stylish
deference. She'll pays his bills,
formulate obligations for
calligraphers (marks, only marks),
marking bodies. Their ineptitude is
deep. Those who cannot reason
with her stated need
organize themselves in shame.

To admire herself. The young
look quickly and away. The elders
cannot grant what she conceives
her need. Graced in black, her
body is a record of her work.
She could not act until her room
was empty: none was left to watch.
Ordered by desire, her fingers
move.  Yet pleasure isn't hers to give.
The door she chose is shut.

## Undulating Light

In this work emanating light,
the line projects from the canvas
so that stability (our icon) is undone.

Photographs disguise themselves
as bustling boys, rude innocents
in lands of metal touched by rust.
This figuration makes us see ourselves
as crude again,
                        as we are.

Lines from the canvas jut.
Galleries leave us
alone, corrupted, at rest,
sought as the symbol
of an art now conscious of itself,
as burst icon, fragment, line, soft and
touchable, winding through the self
like spidery silk,
a liquid silk.

A second sight! Bustling, as persistent
as this emboldened rose, fraternal,
but only with permission: touch.

# Unlike Our Men of Substance, Fattened for the Kill

Every disciple a chip,
mind without mind, you are
a python beside the stream,
lazy, alert,
docile, alone.

We're drawn to infected pools, you and I,
where what we take is what we want.
Predators leap. We wish to kill
before they kill. Predators prey.

The mind is translucent glass:
the mist that owns the tree
owns even fraud.
Nothing escapes the mind
of a poet.

# WALL STREET WEST: THE BOARD OF DIRECTORS

Heretics can't redeem
the answers business taught.
The ferocity of fat cats
leaves no hope except their own.
They may dissent from what
they used to know.
They gather storms from banks
and beg for nothing but another
want. They're born to rule.

## We Did What We Like

How many memories,
except the long walk to his room,
has he left behind? We can't talk now about
what can't be seen, not now. Reason
shifts. It won't hold still.
The images we conjure
date from childhood.
Then we could believe.

The light crossed fields and reached the lawn.
The elderly were not alone.
Children had to find their way back home.
Some disappeared.
They lost their way.
The rest of us knew mystery:
the bread, the word.
We knew
desire, touch.
We're no more worthy just because we say
the name, not now.
Back then, we found
the word a trespass, a flurry, false,
until the sky was blue, a blur.
Answers came to questions we could phrase,
obedient and wanting you.

A flash streaks by,
perhaps an airplane, barely seen.
When we were children,
we felt we had the right to know.

## Wedding Tableau

First, reverse your feelings as you shut the door.
The wedding is a dress, bouquets, and cloistered light.
The windows open like a franchise at the mall.

I pretend it never went like this.
Shut the door.
Fathom how we swim toward light.

Poems were glissando
when you were still my friend.
Afternoons were cheap.

I found that promises were
better than your mouth.

Garçon! My lover needs a drink.

## Within this Room

Pleasure breeds
your touch
without its thought.

Young men become
as certain
as the sun.
I reach their softness
when I study them.

Their wall is hard,
does not recall,
does not record.

The windows once were open.
I move today in spectral light.
I have no sun.

Outside (I know) the leaves are crisp
and blue. The air is slick with eyes,
discontent, unreasoned, wrong.

We learned to touch, to smooth
where no one else
either can or will.

Who's left to see
how long
I linger here?

## WITHOUT OTHERS *(Why We Go On)*

This time, we have the image, and that's all.
This mirror intimating what we've left behind:
the young man on the diving board,
the young man pumping gas.
Do you remember them?

The image, and that's all.

Some have told you secrets,
as if a god could float above your hand,
as if that night the waiter were more than seen.
Remember him, but touching will not be.

Who'd want that, truly? Many do,
and so reduce their words to what they've seen,
no more. No tricks of syntax,
nothing more.

Did he who worked his station
give you more than thanks? There was
a word perhaps, something more.
Tell me why he smiled.

That waiter, too, and all those like him
on the street. Inductive reasoning
says it's best to have a
a secret closet, category, box.

Restrict the image to
unchanging things you feel
if they're in vogue.
Adjust your hair.

The mirror is a fact
that doesn't change.

## Whose Home?

1.
Why can't the looking
end?

Desire's not a pleasure
when it corners you
in empty lots and
busy stores.

And yet it is a blessing.

2.
You're always getting
younger looks
(sly glances)
from those who look so like
the ones you've seen before.

But don't respond.
Buckle down.
Look severe.

3.
Our culture in
these states
binds us to believe
we're free.

Not so.

Boys bolted shut
the doors to satisfaction
years ago.

## Why We Go Away
*for C. H.*

Hear the story of my friend who went away,
leaving kisses, bills, salty moments, secrets in deep cushions.
Who was he?

       Why did he tell me
what he'd done? Silence would have been welcome.
His words were blizzards in a lustrous night.
He was finicky, though answered well
and always laughed, knowing
(this he, just this he)
that when you want the person, give no gift,
or promise. From them, expect no perfect motion,
as in verse, paying back what's due.

February's always grim.
Watch snow.

## ZONE OF INQUIRY

We question a modern *philosophe*.
He speaks the Word within whatever
science might recall. We like his face,
his fingers, how he shifts his feet.
We think we'd like to sleep with him,
but as he speaks, we're forced
to strain with fear.

His thinking leaves us cold.
Though human, he believes analogy
gives the sense of what is known.
Struggling, straightening, regaining
ordered ground,
he tells us anger cannot solve
what physics did.
Excuse? we say. Physics *did!*
Our confidence revives (a bad sign:
we should never trust ourselves).
He shifts his feet.

We withdraw.
Dissident, his verbs
are simply verbs.

## Zooplankton

It's too late.
You were careless.
I will not leave.

I will enter your answers,
and when you speak,
the sounds will be your sounds,
but I will be their cause.

I will retain the easy grace
your folded hands allow.
Your hands will be mine.

# After the Fact; The Elderly Russian Ends His Dance: A Sarabande

*for Ian, when he's older*

Movies gave us hope.
If others lived like this,
why shouldn't we?

\*

We have
nobility, but not quite yet.
We have
too much to which we might return.

\*

Images grow old.
Their stories tell themselves
to others now.

\*

We might tell secrets
with what little's left.
My friend was here.

\*

But not the right occasion.
The more we can withdraw,
the harder truth is felt.

\*

An image tells itself
its own resolve.

*

Memory opens windows
that were never there.

*


Time returns when it is not.
I will look for him,
at least for now,
and hold to that.

Edward Foster's most recent book is *The Beginning of Sorrows*. His selected poems, *What He Ought To Know*, appeared in 2007 He is the author or editor of many books of poetry, biography, and criticism and is a professor of American Studies in the College of Arts and Letters at the Stevens Institute of Technology.

author photo by Arkadii Dragomoshchenko

# PLAYLIST

Y si quieres escuchar lo mejor del grupo, puedes acceder a este enlace:

https://open.spotify.com/user/badmusic/playlist/6AO2uJkrbHnKorrYVnXu0Y

PURPLEMANIA

# MA NON TROPPO - Las novelas del Rock

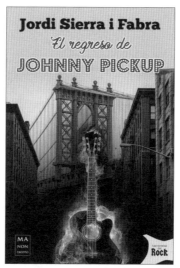

**Un auténtico clásico:**
**una sátira feroz y despiadada del mundo del disco y sus engranajes**

Redbook ediciones y su sello Ma Non Troppo, comprometidos en la divulgación de la música, se ha propuesto la recuperación de libros en el ámbito de la ficción que tengan como trasfondo el mundo del rock en su nueva colección *Las novelas del rock*. Obras nuevas y otras que se descatalogaron en su momento, pero cuyo valor sea innegable como es el caso de esta novela de culto, *El regreso de Johnny Pickup*, del reconocido escritor Jordi Sierra i Fabra. Se trata de una novela que aúna música, nostalgia y humor a partes iguales.

Johnny es un tipo legal, un rockero entre los grandes a quien se le ocurrió la peregrina idea de retirarse a una isla desierta en la Polinesia. A su encuentro acude un crítico musical llamado George Saw que se ha propuesto sacar a Johnny del olvido y volver a Nueva York. Pero Johnny lleva demasiados años retirado, y ni Nueva York es la misma ciudad que conoció, ni el rock ha dejado de evolucionar. Hasta el mismo Dylan se ha convertido al cristianismo. ¿Cómo puede sobrevivir un dinosaurio en un lugar así?

## Otros títulos de Ma non troppo:

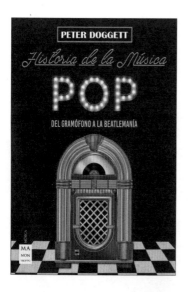

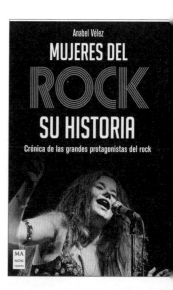